# KEESHOND
# DIARY

## 2020

# *Keeshond Diary 2020*

## Australian Edition

Copyright © 2019 by Shelly Carson & Keera Keeshond

**Acknowledgment:**

*This book is dedicated to animal lovers everywhere.*

*Keera, the canine model in this diary, is a twelve-year-old Keeshond who enjoys raising money for a local children's Hospital. You can follow her adventures on Instagram:*

*Keera_Keeshond*

*Proceeds from the sale of this Diary will be donated to the Royal Children's Foundation charity. You can track purchases and monies raised on the diaries 4 kids fundraiser page*

*https://give.everydayhero.com/au/diaries4kids*

# *Keera*

## All About Keera

Keera was born in Horsham, Victoria, she came to our family home in Melbourne as a young puppy. Keera was puppy number 4 of 6. An absolute gem of a puppy, Keera has a truly lovable character. She is affectionate and loves everyone!!

Keera became a local celebrity when a young boy in the local park stopped dead in his tracks yelling; "Wow! This dog has Harry Potter's glasses!".

Sadly, at age 8, Keera became sick with liver cancer. The fantastic team at the SouthPaws Specialty Surgery and her internal medicine specialist Linda Abraham helped her through her surgery and continuous care. Months later, Keera had two benign tumors removed from her paw and then finally she had a rough run when vets thought Keera needed her tail amputated. Once again, the SouthPaws Specialty Surgery came to the rescue, and no damaged was done.

Keera is now a happy, healthy 12-year-old girl who loves biscuits, her own portable fan, and sleep-ins!!! Our little angel...


Keera's family.

Time is set to Coordinated Universal Time Zone (UT±0)

To convert to

Australian Eastern Standard Time (AEST; UTC+**10:00**)

or during daylight savings:

Australian Eastern Standard Time (AEST; UTC+**11:00**)

# January

**Mon 30**

**Tues 31**

**Wed 1**
New Year's Day (National)

**Thurs 2**

# January

### Fri 3
First Quarter Moon in Aries. 4.45 UTC.
Quadrantids Meteor Shower. Jan 1st-5th. Peaks night of Jan 3rd.

### Sat 4

### Sun 5

### Notes

# January

**Mon 6**

**Tues 7**

**Wed 8**

Devonport Cup (TAS)

**Thurs 9**

# January

## Fri 10
Full Moon in Cancer. Buck Moon. 19:21 UTC.
Penumbral Lunar Eclipse.

## Sat 11

## Sun 12

## Notes

# January

**Mon 13**

**Tues 14**

**Wed 15**

**Thurs 16**

# January

**Fri 17**

Last Quarter Moon in Libra. 12.58 UTC.

**Sat 18**

**Sun 19**

**Notes**

# January

**Mon 20**

**Tues 21**

**Wed 22**

**Thurs 23**

# January

## Fri 24
New Moon in Capricorn. 21:42 UTC.

## Sat 25

## Sun 26
Last Quarter Moon in Scorpio.  21.10 UTC.
Australia Day

## Notes

# January

**Mon 27**
Australia Day Holiday (National)

**Tues 28**

**Weds 29**

**Thurs 30**

# January/February

**Fri 31**

**Sat 1**

**Sun 2**

First Quarter Moon in Taurus. 1.42 UTC.

**Notes**

# February

**Mon 3**

**Tues 4**

**Weds 5**

**Thurs 6**

# February

**Fri 7**

**Sat 8**

**Sun 9**

Full Moon in Leo. Sturgeon Moon. 7:33 UTC. The first supermoon for 2020.

**Notes**

# February

## Mon 10
Mercury at largest Eastern Elongation.
Royal Hobart Regatta (TAS)

## Tues 11

## Weds 12

## Thurs 13

# February

**Fri 14**

Valentine's Day

**Sat 15**

Last Quarter Moon in Scorpio. 22.17 UTC.

**Sun 16**

**Notes**

# February

## Mon 17

## Tues 18
Mercury Retrograde begins.

## Weds 19

## Thurs 20

# February

**Fri 21**

**Sat 22**

**Sun 23**

New Moon in Aquarius. 15:32 UTC.

**Notes**

# February

## Mon 24

## Tues 25

Pancake Day

## Weds 26

Launceston Cup (TAS)
Ash Wednesday

## Thurs 27

# February/March

**Fri 28**

**Sat 29**

**Sun 1**

**Notes**

# March

## Mon 2
First Quarter Moon in Gemini. 19.57 UTC.
Labor Day (WA)

## Tues 3
King Island Show (TAS)

## Weds 4

## Thurs 5

# March

**Fri 6**

**Sat 7**

**Sun 8**

**Notes**

# March

## Mon 9

Full Moon in Virgo, Supermoon. Harvest Moon. 17:48 UTC.
Mercury Retrograde ends.
Labor Day (VIC) Canberra Day (ACT) March Public Holiday (SA)
Eight Hours Day (TAS)

## Tues 10

## Weds 11

## Thurs 12

# March

**Fri 13**

**Sat 14**

**Sun 15**

**Notes**

# March

## Mon 16
Last Quarter Moon in Sagittarius. 9.34 UTC.

## Tues 17
St Patrick's Day

## Wed 18

## Thurs 19

# March

**Fri 20**

March Equinox. 3:50 UTC.

**Sat 21**

**Sun 22**

**Notes**

# March

## Mon 23

## Tues 24

Mercury at most substantial Western Elongation.
Venus at most substantial Eastern Elongation.
New Moon in Aries. 9:28 UTC.

## Weds 25

## Thurs 26

# March

**Fri 27**

**Sat 28**

**Sun 29**

**Notes**

# March/April

**Mon 30**

**Tues 31**

**Weds 1**

First Quarter Moon in Cancer. 10.21 UTC.

**Thurs 2**

# April

**Fri 3**

**Sat 4**

**Sun 5**
Palm Sunday

**Notes**

# April

## Mon 6

## Tues 7

## Weds 8
Full Moon in Libra, Supermoon. Hunters Moon. 2:35 UTC.

## Thurs 9

# April

**Fri 10**

Good Friday (National)

**Sat 11**

Easter Saturday (National except for TAS & WA)

**Sun 12**

Easter Sunday (ACT, NSW, QLD & VIC)

**Notes**

# April

## Mon 13
Easter Monday (National)

## Tues 14
Last Quarter Moon in Capricorn. 22.56 UTC.

## Weds 15

## Thurs 16

# April

**Fri 17**

**Sat 18**

**Sun 19**

**Notes**

# April

**Mon 20**

**Tues 21**

**Weds 22**

Lyrids Meteor Shower. April 16th-25th. Peaks night of April 22nd.

**Thurs 23**

New Moon in Taurus. 2:26 UTC.

# April

**Fri 24**

**Sat 25**
Anzac Day (National)

**Sun 26**

**Notes**

# April

**Mon 27**
Anzac Day Holiday (WA)

**Tues 28**

**Weds 29**

**Thurs 30**
First Quarter Moon in Leo. 20.38 UTC.

# May

Fri 1

Sat 2

Sun 3

Notes

# May

## Mon 4
May Day (NT)
Labor Day (QLD)

## Tues 5

## Weds 6
Eta Aquarids Meteor Shower. April 19th to May 28th. Peaks night of May 6th.

## Thurs 7
Full Moon in Scorpio, Supermoon. Beaver Moon. 10:45 UTC. This is the last of four supermoons for 2020.

# May

### Fri 8
AGFEST (TAS)

### Sat 9

### Sun 10
Mother's Day

### Notes

# May

**Mon 11**

**Tues 12**

**Weds 13**

**Thurs 14**
Last Quarter Moon in Aquarius. 14.03 UTC.

# May

**Fri 15**

**Sat 16**

**Sun 17**

**Notes**

# May

**Mon 18**

**Tues 19**

**Weds 20**

**Thurs 21**

# May

## Fri 22
New Moon in Taurus. 17:39 UTC.

## Sat 23

## Sun 24

## Notes

# May

**Mon 25**

**Tues 26**

**Weds 27**

**Thurs 28**

# May

**Fri 29**

**Sat 30**

First Quarter Moon in Virgo. 3.30 UTC.

**Sun 31**

**Notes**

# June

## Mon 1

Reconciliation Day (ACT)
Western Australia Day (WA)

## Tues 2

## Weds 3

## Thurs 4

Mercury at Greatest Eastern Elongation.

# June

## Fri 5

Full Moon in Sagittarius. Cold Moon. 19:12 UTC.
Penumbral Lunar Eclipse.

## Sat 6

## Sun 7

## Notes

# June

## Mon 8
Queen's Birthday. (National except for QLD & WA)

## Tues 9

## Weds 10
Jupiter at Opposition.

## Thurs 11

# June

**Fri 12**

**Sat 13**
Last Quarter Moon in Pisces. 6.24 UTC.

**Sun 14**

**Notes**

# June

## Mon 15

## Tues 16

## Weds 17

Mercury Retrograde begins.

## Thurs 18

# June

## Fri 19

## Sat 20

## Sun 21

New Moon in Cancer. 6:41 UTC.
June Solstice. 21:44 UTC.
Annual Solar Eclipse.

## Notes

# June

**Mon 22**

**Tues 23**

**Weds 24**

**Thurs 25**

# June

## Fri 26

Borroloola Show Day (NT)

## Sat 27

## Sun 28

First Quarter Moon in Libra. 8.16 UTC.

## Notes

# June/July

**Mon 29**

**Tues 30**

**Weds 1**

**Thurs 2**

# July

## Fri 3
Alice Springs Show Day (NT)

## Sat 4

## Sun 5
Full Moon in Capricorn. Wolf Moon 4:44 UTC.
Penumbral Lunar Eclipse.

## Notes

# July

**Mon 6**

**Tues 7**

**Weds 8**

**Thurs 9**

# July

**Fri 10**

Tennant Creek Show Day (NT)

**Sat 11**

**Sun 12**

Last Quarter Moon in Aries. 23.29 UTC.
Mercury Retrograde ends.

**Notes**

.

# July

**Mon 13**

**Tues 14**
Jupiter at Opposition.

**Weds 15**

**Thurs 16**

# July

**Fri 17**
Katherine Show Day (NT)

**Sat 18**

**Sun 19**

**Notes**

# July

## Mon 20
New Moon in Cancer. 17:33 UTC.
Saturn at Opposition.

## Tues 21

## Weds 22
Mercury at Greatest Western Elongation.

## Thurs 23

# July

**Fri 24**
Darwin Show Day (NT)

**Sat 25**

**Sun 26**

**Notes**

# July/August

**Mon 27**

First Quarter Moon in Scorpio. 12.32 UTC.

**Tues 28**

Delta Aquarids Meteor Shower. July 12th – Aug 23rd. Peaks night of July 28th.

**Weds 29**

**Thurs 30**

# July/August

**Fri 31**

**Sat 1**

**Sun 2**

**Notes**

# August

## Mon 3
Full Moon in Aquarius. Hunger Moon. 15:59 UTC.
Picnic Day (NT)

## Tue 4

## Wed 5

## Thurs 6

# August

Fri 7

Sat 8

Sun 9

Notes

# August

## Mon 10

## Tues 11

Last Quarter Moon in Taurus. 16.45 UTC.

## Weds 12

Perseids Meteor Shower. July 17th - Aug 24th. Peaks night of Aug 12th.
Ekka Wednesday (QLD)

## Thurs 13

Venus at Greatest Western Elongation.

# August

**Fri 14**

**Sat 15**

**Sun 16**

**Notes**

# August

**Mon 17**

**Tues 18**

**Weds 19**

New Moon in Leo. 2:41 UTC.

**Thurs 20**

# August

**Fri 21**

**Sat 22**

**Sun 23**

**Notes**

# August

## Mon 24

## Tues 25
First Quarter Moon in Scorpio. 17.58 UTC.

## Weds 26

## Thurs 27

# August

**Fri 28**

**Sat 29**

**Sun 30**

**Notes**

---

**Mon 31**

---

**Tues 1**

---

**Weds 2**

Full Moon in Pisces. Worm Moon. 5:22 UTC.

---

**Thurs 3**

---

# September

**Fri 4**

**Sat 5**

**Sun 6**
Father's Day

**Notes**

# September

**Mon 7**

**Tues 8**

**Weds 9**

**Thurs 10**

Last Quarter Moon in Gemini. 9.26 UTC.

# September

**Fri 11**

Neptune at Opposition.

**Sat 12**

**Sun 13**

**Notes**

# September

**Mon 14**

**Tues 15**

**Weds 16**

**Thurs 17**

New Moon in Virgo. 11:00 UTC.

# September

**Fri 18**

**Sat 19**

**Sun 20**

**Notes**

# September

## Mon 21

## Tues 22
September Equinox. 13:31 UTC.

## Weds 23

## Thurs 24
First Quarter Moon in Capricorn. 1.55 UTC.

# September

Fri 25

Sat 26

Sun 27

Notes

## Mon 28
Queen's Birthday (WA)

## Tues 29

## Weds 30

## Thurs 1
Full Moon in Aries. Pink Moon. 21:05 UTC.
Mercury at Greatest Eastern Elongation.

# October

### Fri 2
Burnie Show (TAS)

### Sat 3

### Sun 4

### Notes

# October

## Mon 5

Labour Day (ACT, NSW & SA)
Queen's Birthday (QLD)

## Tues 6

## Weds 7

Draconids Meteor Shower. Oct 6th-10th. Peaks night of Oct 7th.

## Thurs 8

Royal Launceston Show (TAS)

# October

**Fri 9**

**Sat 10**

Last Quarter Moon in Cancer. 0.39 UTC.

**Sun 11**

**Notes**

# October

**Mon 12**

**Tues 13**

Mercury Retrograde begins.

**Weds 14**

**Thurs 15**

# October

### Fri 16
New Moon in Libra. 19:31 UTC.
Flinders Island Show (TAS)

### Sat 17

### Sun 18

### Notes

# October

**Mon 19**

**Tues 20**

**Weds 21**

Orionids Meteor Shower. Oct 2nd - Nov 7th. Peaks night of Nov 21st.

**Thurs 22**

Royal Hobart Show (TAS)

# October

**Fri 23**

First Quarter Moon in Capricorn. 13.23 UTC.

**Sat 24**

**Sun 25**

**Notes**

# October

**Mon 26**

**Tues 27**

**Weds 28**

**Thurs 29**

# October/November

## Fri 30

## Sat 31

Full Moon, Blue Moon in Taurus. Flower Moon. 14:49 UTC.
Uranus at Opposition.
Halloween.

## Sun 1

## Notes

# November

### Mon 2
Recreation Day (TAS)

### Tues 3
Mercury Retrograde ends.
Melbourne Cup Day (VIC)

### Weds 4
Taurids Meteor Shower. Sept 7th - Dec 10th. Peaks night of Nov 4th.

### Thurs 5

# November

**Fri 6**

**Sat 7**

**Sun 8**

Last Quarter Moon in Leo. 13.46 UTC.

**Notes**

# November

**Mon 9**

**Tues 10**

**Weds 11**

**Thurs 12**

# November

**Fri 13**

**Sat 14**

**Sun 15**
New Moon in Scorpio. 5:07 UTC.

**Notes**

# November

## Mon 16

## Tues 17

Leonids Meteor Shower. Nov 6$^{th}$-30$^{th}$. Peaks night of Nov 17$^{th}$.

## Weds 18

## Thurs 19

# November

**Fri 20**

**Sat 21**

**Sun 22**

First Quarter Moon in Pisces. 4.45 UTC.

**Notes**

# November

**Mon 23**

**Tues 24**

**Weds 25**

**Thurs 26**

# November

**Fri 27**

Devonport Show (TAS)

**Sat 28**

**Sun 29**

**Notes**

## Mon 30

Full Moon in Gemini. Corn Moon. 9:30 UTC.
Penumbral Lunar Eclipse.

## Tues 1

## Weds 2

## Thurs 3

# December

**Fri 4**

**Sat 5**

**Sun 6**

**Notes**

# December

**Mon 7**

**Tues 8**

Last Quarter Moon in Virgo. 0.37 UTC.

**Weds 9**

**Thurs 10**

# December

**Fri 11**

**Sat 12**

**Sun 13**

Geminids Meteor Shower. Dec 7th-17th. Peaks the nights of Dec 13th-15th.

**Notes**

# December

**Mon 14**

New Moon in Sagittarius. 16:17 UTC.

**Tues 15**

**Weds 16**

**Thurs 17**

# December

**Fri 18**

**Sat 19**

**Sun 20**

**Notes**

# December

## Mon 21

Ursids Meteor Shower. Dec 17th – 25th. Peaks night of Dec 21st.
Great Conjunction of Jupiter and Saturn. December Solstice. 10:02 UTC.
First Quarter Moon in Pisces. 23.41 UTC

## Tues 22

## Weds 23

## Thurs 24

Christmas Eve (SA)

# December

### Fri 25

Christmas Day (National)

### Sat 26

Boxing Day (National except for SA)
Proclamation Day (SA)

### Sun 27

### Notes

# December

## Mon 28

Boxing Day Holiday (National except for SA)
Proclamation Day Holiday (SA)

## Tues 29

## Weds 30

Full Moon in Cancer. Strawberry Moon. 3:28 UTC.

## Thurs 31

New Year's Eve (SA)

## About Diaries 4 Kids

The Diaries featured in this series raise important funds for the Royal Melbourne Children's Hospital Foundation. You help create a brighter future for sick children by purchasing this Diary.
Titles in this series are:

**Keeshond Diary 2020**
**Pomeranian Diary 2020**

You can follow the fundraising efforts on Everyday Hero
https://give.everydayhero.com/au/diaries4kids

The proceeds that the author raises from the sales of this diary will be donated to this fundraising page.

Thank you for your support.

## Keera's
## first day home and at 9 months of age.

*May dogs run freely in your world in 2020, and beyond.*

www.ingramcontent.com/pod-product-compliance
Lightning Source LLC
Chambersburg PA
CBHW051444280526
45785CB00003B/1427